FOR OUR CHILDREN:

A book to benefit the Pediatric AIDS Foundation

·FOR·OUR· CHILDREN

With illustrations by

JAN BRETT
ERIC CARLE
PAT CUMMINGS
BRUCE DEGEN
TOMIE DE PAOLA
RICHARD EGIELSKI
MORDICAI GERSTEIN
EDWARD GOREY
RODNEY ALAN GREENBLAT
MICHAEL HAGUE
THACHER HURD
WILLIAM JOYCE
STEVEN KELLOGG
DAVID MACAULAY
BARRY MOSER
JERRY PINKNEY
ALICE & MARTIN PROVENSEN
MARC SIMONT
DIANE STANLEY
CHRIS VAN ALLSBURG
DAVID WIESNER
AUDREY WOOD
DON WOOD
PAUL O. ZELINSKY

A book to benefit the Pediatric AIDS Foundation

For Our Children: A book to benefit the Pediatric AIDS Foundation is published by Disney Press, a subsidiary of The Walt Disney Company, 500 South Buena Vista Street, Burbank, California 91521.
Copyright © 1991 The Walt Disney Company

Book design by Edward Miller.
Jacket art by Ariel Glaser.
Music Copying by Christina Davidson.

Copyrights for the individual lyrics and illustrations appear on page 55.

Once upon a time there was a little girl named Ariel. Just as your mother and father think you are very special, her father and I thought she was the most beautiful child in the world.

When Ariel was three years old, her brother, Jake, was born. From the beginning, Ariel knew they would be best friends. As Jake grew, they played together a lot, marveling at the colors in the rainbows, the hidden life in the soil, and the secret faces in the flowers. As the sun set and the stars came out, we looked forward to our favorite part of the day, the time we all cuddled in bed and read a book or listened to music.

One day, Ariel didn't feel well, and after some time the doctors realized that she was sick with something they couldn't make better. Ariel had a disease called AIDS.

Ariel was very brave. Even though she couldn't do everything she could before like run and jump, she and Jake played other games. They would find dandelions to wish on or dress up in old clothes. Sometimes they would just sit together. When Ariel didn't feel well, her friends would visit and together they would laugh and smile. She loved a special song she heard on television that made her laugh more than anything. It had a funny name, "Jellyman Kelly," and a singer named James Taylor sang it.

One day, someone told James Taylor that Ariel was sick and that she loved his funny song. He sang "Jellyman Kelly" and other happy songs on a tape and sent it to Ariel as a very special present. Whenever Ariel didn't feel well, she listened to the tape and it made her smile.

Ariel, Jake, her father, and I loved each other every day. But, one day, Ariel died. Then we had to find her smile in other places—in the rainbows, in the clouds, in the flowers, and, most of all, in loving each other.

Remembering how happy songs and books made Ariel, we told our story about being a family with AIDS to the people at Walt Disney Records. They decided to make a special album of songs. James Taylor and many other people decided to be a part of the album because they know what you probably know too, that it feels good to help other people.

When Disney Publishing heard about the album, they also wanted to help, and so they put together this book. The money raised by selling the book and record will help find answers so doctors will know what to do for other children with pediatric AIDS.

This book, like a flower, grew out of caring and blossomed with love. All who contributed to it and all who read it help bring hope to many children like Ariel around the world.

One of the songs in the book says…

> *We have to give a little love*
> *Have a little hope*
> *Make this world a little better.*
> *Try a little more*
> *Harder than before*
> *Let's see what we can do together.*

And that is what you are doing now.

Ariel, her brother, Jake, her dad, all their friends at the
Pediatric AIDS Foundation, and I thank you for helping us
to find smiles and hope together.

Elizabeth Glaser

F or Our Children was originally conceived when James Taylor created a tape of songs especially for Ariel Glaser. After Ariel's death from AIDS - related illness, her mother, Elizabeth Glaser, approached Walt Disney Records with the idea for a compilation album to benefit the Pediatric AIDS Foundation. The album received heartwarming support from many of today's most talented musicians. The recording artists donated their time and each performed a song for the album—some classics and some recorded especially for *For Our Children*. The lyrics for each of these songs, except Elton John's specially created instrumental song, "The Pacifier," are included in *For Our Children: A book to benefit the Pediatric AIDS Foundation*. We have also included the musical notation for piano and guitar for five of the melodies. They have been selected because they represent a variety of styles, are accessible to children of different ages, and are not easily found elsewhere. The lyrics are presented here as performed on the album, in the singular style of each artist. They are

"Goodnight, My Love (Pleasant Dreams)"   Paula Abdul
"Tell Me Why"   Pat Benatar
"The Ballad of Davy Crockett"   Stephen Bishop
"This Old Man"   Bob Dylan
"Medley of Rhymes"   Debbie Gibson
"Child of Mine"   Carole King
"Itsy Bitsy Spider"   Little Richard
"Give a Little Love"   Ziggy Marley
"Blueberry Pie"   Bette Midler

"Mary Had a Little Lamb"	Paul McCartney
"Blanket for a Sail"	Harry Nilsson
"Chicken Lips and Lizard Hips"	Bruce Springsteen
"Gartan Mother's Lullaby"	Meryl Streep
"A Child Is Born"	Barbra Streisand
"Autumn to May"	Ann and Nancy Wilson
"Golden Slumbers"	Jackson Browne
	and Jennifer Warnes
"Getting to Know You"	James Taylor
"Cushie Butterfield"	Sting
"Country Feelin's"	Brian Wilson

As the album neared completion, Disney Juvenile Publishing approached some of the finest and most well-loved children's book artists and asked them to donate a new or previously created illustration for a song on the album. The response was overwhelming. The artists who gave of their time created a book filled with the spirit of giving and sharing.

Here are the collective efforts of many generous contributors.

TABLE OF CONTENTS

GOODNIGHT, MY LOVE

(Pleasant Dreams)

oodnight, my love
Goodnight, my love

Goodnight, my love
Pleasant dreams and sleep tight my love
May tomorrow be sunny and bright
And bring you closer to me

Before you go
There's just one thing I want to know
Is your love still warm for me
Or has it gone cold?

If you should awake
In the still of the night
Please have no fears
I'll be there
You know I care
Please give your love to me, dear

Goodnight, my love
Goodnight, my love

TELL ME WHY

*T*ell me why the stars do shine
Tell me why the ivy twines
Tell me why the sky's so blue
And then I'll tell you just why I love you

Because God made the stars to shine
Because God made the ivy twine
Because God made the sky so blue
Because God made you that's why I love you

Tell me why the stars do shine
Tell me why the ivy twines
Because God made the sky so blue
Because God made you that's why I love you

Tell — me why — the stars do shine, — Tell — me

why — the i - vy twines, — Tell — me why — the

sky's so blue, — And then I'll tell you just why I love you.

THE BALLAD OF DAVY CROCKETT

*B*orn on a mountain top in Tennessee
Greenest state in the land of the free
Raised in the woods, so he knew every tree
Killed him a b'ar when he was only three

Davy, Davy Crockett, the man who don't know fear
Davy, Davy Crockett, king of the wild frontier

Fought single-handed through the Injun wars
Till the Creeks was whipped and the peace was in store
While he was handling this risky chore
Made himself a legend forevermore

Davy, Davy Crockett, holding his promise dear
Davy, Davy Crockett…

Went off to Congress and served a spell
Fixing up the government and laws as well
Took over Washington, so I hear tell
And patched up the crack in the Liberty Bell

Davy, Davy Crockett, seeing his duty clear
Davy, Davy Crockett, king of the wild frontier

He give his word and he give his hand
His Injun friends could keep their land
The rest of his life he took the stand
That justice was due every redskinned man

Davy, Davy Crockett, holding his promise dear
Davy, Davy Crockett, king of the wild frontier

THIS OLD MAN

*T*his old man, he played one
He played knick-knack on my drum

Chorus
With a knick-knack, patty-whack,
give the dog a bone
This old man came rolling home

This old man, he played two
He played knick-knack on my shoe
Chorus
This old man, he played three
He played knick-knack on my knee
Chorus
This old man, he played four
He played knick-knack on my door
Chorus
This old man, he played five
He played knick-knack on my hive
Chorus
This old man, he played six
He played knick-knack on my sticks
Chorus
This old man, he played seven
He played knick-knack up to heaven
Chorus
This old man, he played eight
He played knick-knack on my plate
Chorus
This old man, he played nine
He played knick-knack on my spine
Chorus
This old man, he played ten
He played knick-knack now and then
Chorus

MEDLEY OF RHYMES

MAN IN THE MOON

The man in the moon
Looked out of the moon
Looked out of the moon and said
'Tis time for all children on the earth
To think about getting to bed

TWINKLE, TWINKLE, LITTLE STAR

Twinkle, twinkle, little star
How I wonder what you are
Up above the world so high
Like a diamond in the sky
Twinkle, twinkle, little star
How I wonder what you are

THREE BLIND MICE

Three blind mice
Three blind mice
See how they run
See how they run
They all ran after the farmer's wife
She cut off their tails with a carving knife
Did you ever see such a sight in your life as
Three blind mice

HUSH LITTLE BABY

Hush little baby don't say a word
Papa's gonna buy you a mocking bird
If the mocking bird won't sing
Papa's gonna buy you a diamond ring
If that diamond ring turns to brass
Papa's gonna buy you a looking-glass
If the looking-glass gets broke
Papa's gonna buy you a billy goat
If that billy goat runs away
Papa's gonna buy another today

CHILD OF MINE

lthough you see the world different than me
Sometimes I can touch upon the wonders that you see
All the new colors in pictures you've designed
Oh, yes, sweet darlin', so glad you are a child of mine

Child of mine, child of mine
Oh, yes, sweet darlin', so glad you are a child of mine

You don't need direction, you know which way to go
And I don't want to hold you back, I just want to watch you
   grow
You're the one who taught me you don't have to look behind
Oh, yes, sweet darlin', so glad you are a child of mine

Child of mine, child of mine
Oh, yes, sweet darlin', so glad you are a child of mine

Nobody's gonna kill your dreams
Or tell you how to live your life
There'll always be people to make it hard for awhile
But you'll change their heads when they see you smile

The times you were born in may not have been the best
But you can make the times to come better than the rest
I know you will be honest if you can't always be kind
Oh, yes, sweet darlin', so glad you are a child of mine

Child of mine, child of mine
Oh, yes, sweet darlin', so glad you are a child of mine

*T*he itsy bitsy spider went up the water spout
Down came the rain and washed the spider out
Out came the sun and dried up all the rain
And the itsy bitsy spider went up the spout again

The itsy bitsy spider up the water spout
Down come the rain and washed the spider out
Yo, out come the sun and dried all the rain
Now the itsy

Yo, yo, yo, yo, he did not try again
But he did

Yo, yo, yo, yo, he did not try again
But he did

He tried, he tried
He tried, he tried

He tried, he tried
He tried, he tried

Itsy bitsy spider

Itsy bitsy spider

He got an itsy bitsy spider

He got an itsy bitsy spider

Sometime after rain
He knew it did not mean a thing
The spider does too
Cause he knew just what to do
Itsy bitsy spider
Itsy bitsy spider

e got to give a little love
Have a little hope
Make this world a little better
Oh-oh whoah
Oh-oh whoah

Living in this crazy world
So caught up in the confusion
Nothing is making sense
For me and you
Maybe we can find a way
There's got to be a solution
How to make a brighter day
What do we do?

We got to give a little love
Have a little hope
Make this world a little better
Try a little more
Harder, than before
Let's do what we can do together
Oh-oh whoah, whoah-oh
We can even make it better, yeah
Oh-oh, la, la, la
Only if we try

Got the wars on our minds
Got the troubles on our shoulders
Sometimes it seems so much
What we go through
Maybe if we take the time
Time to understand each other
We can learn to make it right
What do we do?

We got to give a little love
Have a little hope
Make this world a little better
Try a little more
Harder than before
Let's do what we can do together
Oh-oh whoah, whoah-oh
We can even make it better, yeah
Oh-oh, la, la, la
Only if we try

If everybody took somebody by the hand
Someone take 'em by the hand
Maybe everyone could learn to
love and understand

Oh-whoah
We can really make it better, yeah
Oh-whoah, la, la, la
Only if we try
Sing it!
Oh-whoah, la, la, la
We can really make it better, yeah
Only if we try

We got to give a little love
Have a little hope
Make this world a little better
Try a little more
Harder than before
Let's do what we can do together
Oh-oh whoah, whoah-oh
We can even make it better, yeah
Oh-oh, la, la, la
Only if we try

We got to give a little love
Have a little hope
Make this a little better
We could do it together, together
Give a little love
Give a little love
Sing about the love
Sing about the love.

on - ly if __ we __ try. __ (to verse)

If ev - 'ry-bo - dy __ took some - bo - dy by __ the hand __

then may-be ev - 'ry- one __ could learn to love and un-der-stand. Oh whoah

BLUEBERRY PIE

Blueberry Pie, he walks on by
And I don't know what to do
With that Blueberry Pie
But I'm gonna try
Oh Blueberry Pie, sad and shy
Won't you come out of your shell?
Life is swell, so are you!
Please don't be so very blue

Come on Blue! There is a party in your head
Be my friend and we will laugh 'til we turn red!
Want to know why I picked you from the bunch?
You looked so sweet—let's say I had a hunch
That you'd be silly, I'd be silly
We'd be a pair!
Life is peachy, we'll go bananas
No one will care!

Blueberry Pie, let's have fun
'Cause, when all is said and done
I love you, yes I do
'Cause Blueberry, you're true blue!

Blueberry Pie, he's from the upper crust
Rolling in dough, he's half-baked
    and bound to bust!
So don't be flaky, come on now, take me
    to your bakery!
We'll be jamming, ovens slamming, the whole
    world will see

Blueberry me! Without you
There would be no berry pie
Tell me why you can't see you are necessary
Blueberry Pie, let's have fun
'Cause when all is said and done
I love you, yes I do!
'Cause Blueberry, you're true blue!

MARY HAD A LITTLE LAMB

ary had a little lamb
Its fleece was white as snow
And everywhere that Mary went
That lamb was sure to go

And you could hear them singing:
"La la, la la, la la la la la la
La la, la la, la la la la la la"

It followed her to school one day
It was against the rule
It made the children laugh and play
To see a lamb at school

And you could hear them singing:
"La la, la la, la la la la la la
La la, la la, la la la la la la"

And so the teacher turned it out
But still it lingered near
It waited patiently about
Till Mary did appear

And you could hear them singing:
"La la, la la, la la la la la la
La la, la la, la la la la la la"

"Why does the lamb love Mary so?"
The eager children cry
"Why, Mary loves the lamb, you know"
The teacher did reply

And you could hear them singing:
"La la, la la, la la la la la la
La la, la la, la la la la la la"

Moderately slow

Mar-y had a lit-tle lamb, it's fleece was white as snow, and

Ev-'ry-where that Mar-y went, that lamb was sure to go.___

___ and you could hear them sing-ing: La la, La la,

La la la ___ la la la. La la, La la,

La la la ___ la la la.

32

BLANKET FOR A SAIL

ay out on the ocean, far beyond the seven seas
There's a tiny little boat, faith that's keeping her afloat
And a tiny little skipper with his worn and tattered coat

You see, the law of the ocean says you shall never fail
Use your heart as a rudder, faith as a compass
And a blanket for a sail

Sleep for the weary and dreams for us all
Rest your head on a pillow and I'll tell you a tale
Use your heart as a blanket and a blanket for a sail

Way out on the ocean, far beyond the seven seas
There's a tiny little boat, faith that's keeping her afloat
And its tiny little skipper and his worn and tattered coat

You see, the law of the ocean says that you shall never fail
Just use your heart as a rudder, faith as a compass
And a blanket for a sail

Way out on the o-cean _____ far be-yond the sev-en seas ____

____ There's a ti-ny lit-tle boat, faith that's keep-ing her a-float and a

ti-ny lit-tle skip-per with his worn and tat-tered coat. You see the

law of the o-cean _____ says you shall nev-er fail ____

____ use your heart as a rud-der, faith as a com-pass, and a

blan-ket for a sail. _____

CUSHIE BUTTERFIELD

I'm a broken-hearted keelman
And I'm o'er head in love
With a young lass from Gyetsid
And I call 'er my dove

Her name's Cushie Butterfield
And she sells yellow clay
And 'er cousin's a muckman
And they call him Tom Gray

She's a big lass
She's a bonny lass
And she likes her beer
And I call her Cushie Butterfield
And I wish she was here

Her eyes is like two holes
In a blanket burnt through
And her breath in the mornin'
Would scare a young coo

She wears big galoshes
And her stockings once was white
And her bed down it's lilac
And her hat's never straight

CHICKEN LIPS AND LIZARD HIPS

Oh, when I was a little kid
I never liked to eat
Mom would put things on my plate
And I'd dump 'em on her feet
But then one day she made this soup
I ate it all in bed
I asked her what she put in it
And this is what she said:

"Chicken lips and lizard hips
And alligator eyes
Monkey legs and buzzard eggs
And salamander thighs
Rabbit ears and camel rears
And tasty toenail pies
Stir 'em all together
And it's mama's soup surprise"

I went into the bathroom
And I stood beside the sink
I said, "I'm feeling slightly ill
And I think I'd like a drink"

Mama said, "I've just the thing
I'll get it in a wink
It's full of lots of protein
And vitamins, I think"

"Oh, chicken lips and lizard hips
And alligator eyes
Monkey legs and buzzard eggs
And salamander thighs
Rabbit ears and camel rears
And tasty toenail pies
Stir 'em all together
And it's mama's soup surprise"

Oh, when I was a lit-tle kid I nev-er liked to eat

Mom would put things on my plate, and I'd dump 'em on her feet But

then one day___ she made this soup, I ate it all in bed I

asked her what she put in it ___ and this is what she said:

CHORUS:
Chick-en lips and liz-ard hips and al-li-ga-tor eyes

Mon-key legs and buz-zard eggs and sal-a-man-der thighs

Rab-bit ears and cam-el rears and tast-y toe-nail pies

Stir 'em all to-geth-er And it's Ma-ma's Soup Sur-prise.

GARTAN MOTHER'S LULLABY

Sleep, my child, for the red bee hums
The silent twilight falls
Eivell from the gray rock comes
To wrap the world in thralls

And lyin' there, oh, my child, my joy
My love and heart's desire
The crickets sing you a lullaby
Beside the dyin' fire

Dusk has come and the green man's thorn
Is wreathed in rings of fog
Shivrah sails his boat till morn
Along the starry bog

And over it all the paley moon
Has gleamed her cusp in dew
And weeps to hear the sad sleep tune
I sing, oh love, to you

And lyin' there, oh, my child, my joy
My love and heart's desire
The crickets sing you a lullaby
Beside the dyin' fire

A child is born
We suddenly step through a thousand doors
A child is born
Her chin is like mine but her eyes are yours
How perfectly formed are her fingers
So far to reach, so much to know
What worlds will be found by her fingers
We'll hold her close, then let her go
How sweet to find a part of ourselves we
    knew nothing of
A child is born
A child that is born of our love

AUTUMN TO MAY

Oh, once I had a little dog
Her color it was brown
I taught her for to whistle
To sing and dance and run

Her legs, they were fourteen yards long
Her ears so very wide
Around the world in half a day
Upon her I could ride

Sing terrio-day
Sing autumn to May

Oh, once I had a little frog
He wore a vest of red
He'd lean upon a silver cane
A top hat on his head

He'd speak of far-off places
Of things to see and do
And all the kings and queens he met
While sailin' in a shoe

Sing terrio-day
Sing autumn to May

Oh, once I had a flock of sheep
That grazed upon a feather
I'd keep them in a music box
From wind and rainy weather

And every day the sun would shine
They'd fly out through the town
And bring me back some golden rings
And candy by the pound

Sing terrio-day
Sing autumn to May

Oh, once I had a downy swan
She was so very frail
She sat upon an oyster shell
Hatched me out a snail

The snail, it changed into a bird
The bird to butterfly
And he who tells a bigger tale
Will have to tell a lie

Sing terrio-day
Sing autumn to May

GOLDEN SLUMBERS

nce there was a way to get back homeward
Once there was a way to get back home
Sleep pretty darling do not cry
And I will sing a lullaby

Golden slumbers fill your eyes
Smiles awake you when you rise
Sleep pretty darling do not cry
And I will sing a lullaby

Once there was a way to get back homeward
Once there was a way to get back home
Sleep pretty darling do not cry
And I will sing a lullaby

Golden slumbers fill your eyes
Smiles awake you when you rise
Sleep pretty darling do not cry
And I will sing a lullaby

Oh, you're gonna carry that weight
Carry that weight a long time
Oh, you're gonna carry that weight
Carry that weight a long time

Country feelin's, they're a-callin' me and brother I'm
feelin' fine
Wanna cut loose from the city—get out and run around
Country feelin's movin' in my feet and dancin' in
the hot sunshine
I'm gonna spread that country feelin' all around the town

Bamp-b-bamp-bamp-bamp
Bamp-b-bamp-bamp-bamp
Bamp-b-bamp-bamp-bamp
Bamp-b-bamp-bamp-bamp

Country feelin's at a county fair and under a big blue sky
See those prize bulls, cotton candy, red balloons
and an apple pie
Country feelin's puttin' me on top of the world
on this happy day
I'm gonna spread that country feelin' all around the town

Bamp-b-bamp-bamp-bamp
Bamp-b-bamp-bamp-bamp
Bamp-b-bamp-bamp-bamp
Bamp-b-bamp-bamp-bamp

Country, country feelin'
Country, country feelin'
Country, country feelin'
Oh, oh-oh-oh-oh

Country feelin's, they got me sittin' right there in a
rockin' chair
On a porch outside with a cold lemonade and the clean,
fresh air
Stand up tall, be proud of yourself and you just
step out there
I'm gonna spread those country feelin's all around the town
I'm gonna spread that country feelin' all around the town
I'm gonna spread that country feelin' all around the town
I'm gonna spread that country feelin' all around the town

GETTING TO KNOW YOU

etting to know you
Getting to know all about you
Getting to like you
Getting to hope you like me

Getting to know you
Putting it my way, but nicely
You are precisely my cup of tea

Getting to know you
Getting to feel free and easy
When I am with you
Getting to know what to say

Having to notice
Suddenly I'm bright and breezy
Because of all the beautiful and new
Things I'm learning about you
Day by day

Getting to know you
Getting to feel free and easy
When I am with you
Getting to know what to say

Having to notice
Suddenly I'm bright and breezy
Because of all the beautiful and new
Things I'm learning about you
Day by day

Day by day